James Pitcher

The Hermit of Moss Pond

A Romance of the Upper Susquehanna

James Pitcher

The Hermit of Moss Pond
A Romance of the Upper Susquehanna

ISBN/EAN: 9783744673587

Printed in Europe, USA, Canada, Australia, Japan

Cover: Foto ©Thomas Meinert / pixelio.de

More available books at **www.hansebooks.com**

The Hermit

of

= Moss Pond. =

. .

A Romance

of the

Upper Susquehanna,

by

James Pitcher.

. .

Hartwick Seminary, N. Y.,
1896.

Table of Contents.

I.	Introductory,	5
II.	The Wanderer,	19
III.	Joseph Manly,	25
IV.	Disappearance,	33
V.	Agnes Daire,	47
VI.	Walks and Talks,	57
VII.	Defalcation,	85
VIII.	Some Letters,	93
IX.	Decline,	115
X.	School,	123
XI.	The Hermit,	131
XII.	Moss Pond,	137
XIII.	Recognition,	143
XIV.	Graduation,	155
XV.	The Trial,	165
XVI.	Fruition,	181

I.

Introductory.

(The Upper Susquebanna.)

Daily Prayer.

IN the morning, Lord, I pray,
   Grant thy favor through this day;
Help me all my burdens bear,
Shield me from the tempter's snare.

When the day has grown to noon,
Grant thy favor, lest I soon
Heedless be of thy dear love,
While through toils and cares I move.

When my daily task is done,
Grant thy favor, ere the sun,
Hastening in his westward flight,
Drops the sable pall of night.

When mine eyelids close in sleep,
Grant thy favor; o'er me keep
Loving vigil, so I may
Welcome give the new-born day.

1. Introductory.

MIDWAY within the Empire State,—
A commonwealth both rich and great,—
The "Glimmerglass" in beauty lies,
Beneath unrivaled azure skies.

To eastward, in condition still
As when the Redman roamed at will,
Majestic hills rise from the shore,
With virgin forests covered o'er;
While to the westward may be seen
Less rugged hills with vales between,
Whose gentler slopes and richer soil
Reward the farmers' patient toil.

At either end a village lies,
Whence heavenward-pointing steeples rise.
The shore is punctuated round
With camps and cottages, here found,
Which gleam from jutting points among,
Like gems upon a necklace strung.

The waters of this fairy lake
Sometimes a silvery mirror make,
In which the forests, hills and capes
Are reproduced in magic shapes
Of monsters stretched along the shore,
With strange bilateral trappings o'er.

Here from the Natty Bumppo's deck,
Or from the lesser craft that fleck
The glassy surface of the lake,
The pleasure seekers often take
The health-promoting mountain air,
And view the prospects, rich and rare:

Kingfisher Tower at first appears;
The Sleeping Lion next uprears
His stalwart shape against the skies,
Near where the Sunken Island lies.

Or if the travelers are inclined
To more romantic turn of mind,

INTRODUCTORY.

They disembark and visits pay
To Sulphur Springs along the way;
Or Leatherstocking's cave explore;
Or listen to the rythmic roar
Of waters leaping o'er the walls
Of Leatherstocking's magic Falls;
Or if, perchance, sly Cupid be
A member of the company,
And should they seek more quiet nook,
They glide into the Shadow Brook.

My feeble pen might well decline
To sketch the beauties of this shrine;
But 'twere a pity if, perchance,
One who has courage to advance
Thus far with this ambitious lay
Should fail to note this shadowy way.

Where Lake Otsego sweeps around
The Sleeping Lion, may be found
A deep and spacious sheltered bay,
That stretches eastward far away.

Here, from the northward wooded shore,
Into this bay, the waters pour
From placid stream, whose portals lie
Half hidden 'neath the branches nigh.
A boat, howe'er, may safely glide,
Upon this gateway's flowing tide;
And once this tangled wood within,
A lovers' true retreat is seen.

The waters are surprising clear,
In which the sporting fish appear
To frolic, midst the shadows cast,
As over-arching trees are passed.

The bittersweet, and wild grape vine,
And ivy, with each other twine;
And hang in gay festoons above
The watery way in which we move.
Upon the banks we may discern
The rare and graceful walking fern;
And other queer fantastic forms
Of vegetation's sportive charms.

INTRODUCTORY.

The mossy banks are mirrored, too,
And so redoubled to our view;
Birds sing among the trees grown near,
And squirrels chatter, as they hear
The splashing of the boatman's oar.
Sometimes is heard the curious roar
Of frightened partridges.   Sometimes
The azure sky an eagle climbs.

Oft overhanging limbs impend;
And drooping vines so low extend,
That those who would their way pursue,
Must lowly bow, till they are through.
What wonder that of heads a pair
In close proximity oft are?
Nor would it be a thing unheard,
If in such case it has occurred,
That *toll* is sought from first to last,
Whene'er these emerald gates are passed.

At this fair lakelet's southern bound,
A famous village may be found;

Known to the world of fiction wide,
As Templeton,—Otsego's pride;—
Its other name of like renown,
Is, from its founder, COOPERSTOWN.

'Tis not our purpose to outline
This charming literary shrine;
That gracious task might well relate,
To some inspired laureate.

Reluctant though we leave the place,
The tortuous pathway now to trace,
Through mountain glen, or verdured lea,
By which these waters seek the sea.
Nor is it strange that they should yearn,
By mists and vapors to return;
For one who here has dwelt betimes,
Is scarce content with other climes;
But season after season comes
From busy trade or urban homes,
To breathe anew this mountain air,
And sail upon these waters fair.

INTRODUCTORY.

The Susquehanna takes its rise
Here in this rural paradise,
Where *Cooper* made each inch of ground
Both classical and world renowned.
Its mouth five hundred miles away,
Is Chesapeake, an ample bay.
A " Crooked River " 'tis indeed,
True to its name, we are agreed.
And one with reason might surmise,
That, in its onward course, it tries
To spell its name with letters delf,
So oft it doubles on itself.

Here, it is easy quite to span
With rod and line of fisherman;
There, half a league it stretches o'er
Its rocky bed from shore to shore;
And lowing herds are often seen,
Half way its distant banks between;
For though its volume oft is swelled
From floods by tributaries held,

Its banks retire to give it room,
The while its depth is much the same.

Fair cities, towns, and hamlets lie
In rich profusion clustered nigh;
The locomotive's whistle shrill,
Re-echoing from hill to hill,
Gives evidence of industry,
From mountain source to distant sea.
Rich mines of coal long time concealed,
Here in these hills their treasures yield;
The wooded heights alike reward
The axman's toil and wealth afford;
And mile on mile of rafted trees
Sometimes are seen to lie at ease,
Till on some freshet's tumbling roar,
They float to yield their gathered store.

'Tis well to pause, ere we advance,
To note this curious circumstance:
While Lake Otsego is, of course,
The Susquehanna River's source,

Itself is fed by springs, and rills,
And lakelets in surrounding hills.
One of these last it is well known
Divides its waters overflown;
Some running toward Otsego Lake,
And some a northward journey take,
And with the Mohawk finally,
Through lordly Hudson find the sea.
And strangely do these streams compare,—
The one, as we are well aware,
Is long and wide and shallow, too,
And crooked all its journey through;
The other half the length and straight,
But deep and broad,—of service great,
For every kind of water craft,
From panting tug, with lumber raft,
To floating palace here can find
A highway suited to its mind.
So ample is the Hudson's tide,
That largest ships can safely ride;
And here the ensigns be unfurled,
Of all the navies of the world.

Each has its uses, each its charms,
And like a pair of brawny arms,
The one bears up the mighty weight
Of commerce or of human freight;
The other turns the wheels of scores
Of busy factories on its shores.

We hope our friends will not refuse,
This slight digression to excuse;
We now take up our wonted task,
And for our story patience ask.

A league to southward from its source,—
Three times a league by winding course,—
(For whoso would its current trace
All points of compass he must face,)
The Susquehanna's narrow vale
Here widens to an ample dale.
The curious form in which 'tis planned
Is well outlined by human hand:
If dexter member is stretched forth,
Palm up, with digits pointing north,

INTRODUCTORY.

In miniature the hills between,
A broad and level plain is seen.
The thumb is Beaver Meadow's course,
The index is the river's source,
One may the middle valley take
To reach CANADARAGA LAKE,
While lesser vales to westward lie,
And lead to thriving hamlets nigh.

Here at this palmate's western bound
A seat of learning may be found;
Both venerable and far-famed,
And from its founder, HARTWICK named.

To eastward, by the river's side,
Doth white-winged Charity abide;
And minister from ample store,
To the unfortunate and poor.

Somewhat to south of middle ground,
Is rare and curious Indian Mound,
Which like inverted basin lies,
Above an acre as to size.

Sometimes the river overflows,
From vernal rains and melting snows,
When all alone amid the flood,
Bedecked with spotless, snow-white hood,
Among the surging waves, the while,
The Mound is like a fairy isle.
But though it long is known to fame,
And bears a quite suggestive name,
The treasures in its bosom stored,
Were often guessed but ne'er explored.

II.

The Wanderer.

Snow Crystals.

THOU Crystal of Snow, multiform yet six-angled,
    How seldom thy perfect form is our delight;
As jostled by winds, or by wrathful storms mangled,
    Thy wondrous construction is lost to our sight.

Oh wealth of the love of our Father in Heaven,
    To lavish his mercies on us here below;
While heedless we spurn the rich boon he has given,
    As we brush off the beautiful Crystals of Snow.

Snow Crystal, thou poem six-stanzaed, Oh teach me,
    How out of the measureless depths of the sky
Are formed those fantastical visions that reach me,
    A source of unceasing delight to mine eye.

And teach me how out of life's conflicts and duty,
    Its sorrows and trials, its grief and its joy;
My life may be crystalized into rare beauty,
    To gladden the world, in the Master's employ.

11. The Wanderer.

THE eastern hills which parallel
    The river's course, are wooded well;
And here 'tis not uncommon sight
To see above their spired height,
The curling smoke arising high,
From woodman's camp toward wintry sky.

The dwellers in the valley near
So oft had seen this smoke appear,
That no one gave it e'en a thought,
Or for an explanation sought.
A year indeed had quickly passed,
Since sound of axe was noticed last,
The while a curious circumstance
Had no attention claimed, perchance.

In eighteen hundred seventy-five,
On Christmas eve, there did arrive
At this rude camp, 'mid sleet and frost,
A stranger who his way had lost.

He was well clad, of medium height,
Had bright, grey eyes, complexion light,
Smooth face, and hair inclined to curl,
Cheeks fair and rosy as a girl,
And hands well shapen, though inured
To useful toil some time endured.

But as he, trembling, stood before
This now deserted cabin door,
He might be taken for a tramp
Who strayed into this lonely camp;
For scarcely more alive than dead,
Half famished, tired from foot to head,
Late in that bleak December night,
He would have perished save for light
Which at this moment flickered faint,
From embers in a fire-place quaint;
For on that very day, at eve,
The woodsmen did the cabin leave.

When once this shelter was secured,
At thought of what he had endured,

He bowed his weary, aching head,
The while a thankful prayer he said;
Then stirred to life the slumbering fire,
Which helped his courage to inspire.
Some remnant food he soon descried,
Which well his present need supplied.

The long, sad night had nearly passed;
The storm had ceased; and at the last
The stars peeped out and twinkled bright;
The waning moon shed feeble light;
While from the quiver of the sun
The golden arrows had begun
To upward dart, in eastern sky,
To herald that the day was nigh.

Confused as to this lonely spot,
Of its location knowing not,
His most exacting need supplied,
With effort quite extreme he tried
Events to recapitulate,
Which brought him to this wretched state.

A crumpled letter once again
He tried to read, but all in vain.
For, though the fire gave ample light,
His copious tears bedimmed his sight.

Grown drowsy from exhausted strength,
With brief but fervent prayer, at length,
He threw himself upon a cot,
And for a time his woes forgot.

His troubled sleep continued on,
Until the low descending sun
Of Christmas day, its zenith passed;
And, while by sleep he is held fast,
We well may trace the strange events,
Which led up to these sad portents.

III.

Joseph Manly.

Love and Labor.

OH child of mine, that climb'st upon my knee,
    While duties otherwhere my thoughts convey;
I cannot leave my task to fondle thee,
    Nor can I,—dare I,—thrust thee quite away;
Thine arms entwined to stay thy doubtful hold,
My arms not only, but my heart enfold.

Ah! thou mayest never know that what to thee,
    May seem indifference or small desire;
Is but the balance, 'twixt a wealth to me
    Of love and labor, whose half slumbering fire
Needs but the breath of danger, or concern,
Ere quick love's embers with new fervor burn.

So, child of mine, still climb upon my knee,
    E'en though but half a welcome thou secure;
No harsh repellant word shall drive from me
    Thy heart, from every strong temptation pure,
Lest wandering from fond parental sway,
Thy steps forget return,—or lose the way.

III. Joseph Manly.

THE station agent at GREEN CREST
  Was *Joseph Manly*, but addressed
As "Joe,"—a more familiar name;
For when he to the village came,
At once he gained entire respect,
For habits pure and life correct.

An orphan at an early day,
He struggled hard to make his way;
And for some years his rigid rule
Was summer work and winter school;
Till he himself was qualified
At district school-house to preside.

Advancement then more rapid came,
Till a diploma he could claim,
For years of labor diligent,
At Hartwick Seminary spent.

The academic journey done,
The sterner work of life begun;
First as a learner, then relief,
Assistant next, and soon as chief,
In an important inland town,
Along a railway of renown.

Exacting duties were his lot,
But never were his tasks forgot;
And such from childhood was his rule,
His place at church and Sunday-school
Was always filled with reverent pride,
Nor were his services denied;
For soon his latent powers were guessed,
And into service he was pressed,
As teacher of a class of boys,
Whose chief delight was fun and noise.

They were not vicious—not by far—
But pent up boyhood caused a jar
When injudicious rigid rule
Was sternly forced upon the school.

To find a master for this class,
Had seemed their powers to quite surpass;
Till with apology and fear
Was Joe installed as teacher here.

He took the situation in,
Resolved he would at once begin,
Not to suppress the pent up force,
But by controlling guide its course;
For he had learned himself at school,
Of nature this the constant rule:
That water, wind, electric force,
Or steam, or fire, are all the source
Of useful service to our race,
Up to a limit in each case;
But when they are too much confined,
No bands their energies can bind.

Thus Joe devised to study out
What all the members were about;
What sports and games they each preferred;
And if of game of ball he heard,

In which his boys engaged to play,
He happened to be seen that way;
And oft would cheer with hearty glee,
When some good play he chanced to see;
And if an invitation came,
Sometimes he would umpire a game.

If skating party should arise,
He, too, would need some exercise;
And so it happened, through the year,
That Joe in some way would appear,
Connected with their boyish sport,—
But unsuspected the import.

And on the Sabbath, in the class,
No opportunity would pass,
To point a moral for that day,
Somewhat connected with their play;
Till every urchin in the school
Would quote Joe Manly for his rule:
"Joe would do this," and so 'twas right;
And also as conclusive quite,

"This, Joe would never do," 'twas wrong.
So it befell that Joe was strong
In his control of boyish pranks,
For which he had unstinted thanks.

But strangely as it seems to tell,
Joe had his enemies, as well;
For it is doubtful praise if said,
That he no enemies had made;
Defend the right, oppose the wrong,
You meet with opposition strong.
And so the *wise* would nod their head,
And winking say—"You wait, instead!"
"These good young men, 'tis well to watch."
"It takes a thief, a thief to catch!"
"These Christians are, 'tis plain to see,
No better than they ought to be."
"Some scheme he has to gain renown,
And be the idol of the town."

These cruel taunts Joe seldom heard,
Nor had it to his mind occurred

That praise or blame he should deserve,
Because from right he did not swerve.
One rule of conduct he employed:
The right to do, the wrong avoid.

IV.

The Disappearance.

Christmas.

IN Bethlehem's manger, 'mid want and 'mid woe,
The Christ-child was cradled long ages ago;
As Lord of creation, none reigned in his stead;
As Jesus, the Savior, none pillowed his head.

A legion of angels proclaimed at his birth,—
"All glory in heaven, and peace on the earth."
Wise men from the east saw his star in the sky,
And worshiped the babe as the King from on high.

Though ages have passed since that great natal morn,
Each Christmas anew in our hearts he is born;
So now let us offer our hearts undefiled,
To lovingly cradle the blessed Christ-child.

IV. The Disappearance.

SOME time had passed since Joe began
　　His duties as a rail-road man,
And such his strict attention paid
To all the merchants there in trade,
And such his bearing and renown,
He had esteem in all the town.

On Christmas eve the town was shocked,
As people to the churches flocked,
To live again their childish joys,
'Mid Christmas trees, and Christmas toys,
To hear that Joe, whom they revered,
That day had strangely disappeared.

All sorts of reasons were advanced;
The *knowing* at each other glanced;
" I told you so," some ventured now;
And strange it is, I do avow,
How great the millions are, and wise,
To know, invent, foretell, advise,

But just as they would startle all,
With some great product of their skill,
Some wizard genius will arise,
And rudely snatch the valued prize;
And so these self-important seers
Will struggle on for years and years,
To be the favored heirs of fate,
But always just a little late.

"I told you so," will fit each case;
Like oracle, with double face,
The way the issue turns was meant,—
You pay the price and be content.

So now, that clouds Joe's sky o'erspread,
"I knew it all along," they said.
And sceptics sneeringly would cry:
"Another good man gone awry!"
Or, with insinuating glee:
"How much defraud the Company?"
But be it known there were a few,
Who were not moved by this ado;

" 'Tis his misfortune not his blame,
Joe never will belie his name."

At Joe's own church the service lagged;
His class of whom he often bragged,
Were all disconsolate and shy.
With their respected leader nigh,
They would allotted tasks perform,
As though at play, with interest warm;
But like an army without head,
They only were a mob instead.

The organ, too, oft quite sublime,
That night was sadly out of time;
And e'en the pastor's balanced mind,
To wander often seemed inclined.

So like a melancholy pall,
The strange announcement seemed to fall;
Till at the close was offered prayer,
That God would guide the wanderer,

And bring him safe unscathed from sin,
The sheltered fold at last within;
Then tearfully they made their way,
To usher in sad Christmas day.

The while excitement now prevails,
And every explanation fails,
We will return to trace the way
That Joe had spent that wretched day.

That morning early he received
A letter which his spirit grieved;
He read it o'er and o'er again,
To solve the riddle, but in vain;
And as he read his eyes grew dim,
A tremor ran through every limb,
His brain was in a whirl till soon
He fell into a deadly swoon;
And thus unconscious did remain,
Till people came to take the train.

Aroused at last, some thought it queer,
That he so dazed should now appear;
For they supposed he only slept,
From some gay vigil too late kept.

As he went halting to his task,
Some strangers would each other ask,
If from his looks they did not think,
The agent was inclined to drink!

These gibes Joe overheard at length,
Then rallied all his latent strength,
With one supreme resolve to try
Himself to master or to die;
His plans were laid to haste away,
For surely here he could not stay.

The telegraph he put to use,
To ask official quick excuse;
He flashed this message o'er the wire,
Which taxed his feeble strength entire:

"Imperative and instant need
For leave of absence. If agreed,
Send a relief, on Number Three."

The answer came quite speedily:
"O. K., Make full report, for sure,
And send it in on Number Four."

Thus far, at least, did fortune smile;
He bent his energies meanwhile,
To post his books and make report.
He was of such methodic sort,
That ere he left his work each day,
His record was complete alway.

The busy season's added freight
Had swelled the cash receipts of late;
Till several hundred dollars lay
Within the station safe that day.

Just as the eastward bound express
Came to a halt, he wrote address

THE DISAPPEARANCE.

Upon a large envelope sealed,
With " R. R. B." on corner shield;
And was about to hand it o'er,
When he was met at station door,
By messenger from off the train,
Who just a moment did remain,
To have dispatched a message quick;
For he had fallen sorely sick.
Joe took the message, in return
His own exchanged without concern.
The troubled messenger in haste,
Joe's letter in his pocket placed.

" To Mrs. Main,
    At Albany,
Atlantic Street, Five Twenty-three:
Am ill, Send carriage to the train.
On Number Four. On time.
     J. Main.

This message quickly Joe dispatched,
Then for relief impatient watched.

And so absorbed was he in thought,
That e'en his dinner was forgot.

The train at last stood at the door;
The office keys were handed o'er;
But what came next,—where he should go,—
Not having planned, he did not know.

Somehow the summons, "All Aboard!"
The balance of his mind restored,
And matched his present urgent need,
And soon to westward he did speed.

If he had then been asked to tell
His destination; and, as well,
His purpose, it would have been learned,
That he with neither was concerned.
To go away he had prepared,
But whither, neither knew nor cared.

Uncommon it was not to see
Employees riding passage free;

Hence the conductor recognized,
And kindly bowed, nor was surprised;
Except that Joe, he knew not why,
Was not himself, but strangely shy.

The train sped onward in its flight;
The day was waning into night;
When at an old familiar sound,
He waked from lethargy profound.
He tried to rouse his addled brain,
To grasp the name when once again
The brakeman's cry came floating down:
"The JUNCTION, change for COOPERSTOWN."

Joe formed a purpose in a trice:
He would at HARTWICK seek advice.
Well he remembered that at school,
His teachers made it constant rule,
To treat a pupil as a friend,
And guard his interests to the end.
For while his mind had been well drilled,
His soul likewise had been well filled

With reverent counsel for his good,
As he had always understood.

The brakesman's notice seemed command.
Soon as the train came to a stand,
He made the necessary change,
And tried his purpose to arrange;
But ere details had been contrived,
Here at the station he arrived.

When Joe dismounted from the train
A blinding storm of sleet and rain
Had just set in; and from the west,
As he supposed, but wrongly guessed.

Now at this somewhat distant year
There was no station building here;
But those who would a passage gain,
Must by a signal stop the train.

The country round was trackless now,
From fast descending drifting snow.

Joe faced the storm, and made his way
Toward a light, whose flickering ray
Came from a lonely farmhouse found,
To eastward of the Indian Mound.
But he supposed it marked the street
To westward, where his youthful feet
Had often trod the classic halls,
Within his *alma mater's* walls.

First "Russell's Cove" he quickly crossed,
And next the river, bridged with frost;
Then made his way for half a mile,
And greatly wondered that, meanwhile,
His journey should so far extend,
And not already reach an end.
Till he at last was forced to say
That in the storm he'd lost his way,
But where he was, or what to do,
Just then not in the least he knew.

When courage was about to fail,
His weary feet now struck a trail,
Which had been left that very day,
By woodsmen on their homeward way.

This pathway led through a ravine,
Down which sometimes there may be seen,
The tumbling waters from beyond,
Which issue from an ample pond.

This mountain path did Joe ascend ;
He thought that it would somewhere end,
Where shelter could be found, at last,
Until this blinding storm were past.

And so at last it came about,
As has already been found out;
By those whose patience has endured
Until this issue is secured,
That Joe had reached this cabin rude,
Which near Moss Pond to northward stood.

V.

Agnes Daire.

Music (Quatrains.)

I.

THE breath of God, upon the hearts of men,
  Responsive each with tones divinely rare;
As spirit of the harp Æolian,
  Makes answer to the spirit of the air.

II.

The thought of God, conceived and born in heaven,
  But nursed and cradled in the souls of men;
The one employment to us mortals given,
  Which, sundered here, is there resumed again.

III.

The soul's one harpstring, which survives
  The ruin sin in Eden wrought;
A vibrant cord, by which the Father strives
  To re-possess our alien thought.

IV.

A ladder from God's footstool to his seat—
  The King's highway for feet long used to roam;
While Faith, and Hope, and Love, down-climbing, meet
  And convoy new-born souls unto their home.

V. Agnes Daire.

THE thriving village of GREEN CREST
   With thriving churches was well blessed—
The first and largest, Lutheran,
Conducted on such godly plan,
That till the town had largely grown,
It served the worshipers alone;
But later on, with larger size,
Did other steeples grandly rise;
And blend metalic voices clear,
To summon people far and near;
To gather in this earthly shrine,
And render thanks for grace divine.

Of this large church, the Sunday School
Was under the efficient rule
Of Henry Daire of good renown,
A prosperous merchant of the town.

The organist was Agnes Daire,
His only daughter, young and fair;

Reared in a Christian home with care,
No effort did her parents spare,
To train her mind in wisdom's ways,
To fortify 'gainst evil days.

The village school—the village pride—
Her early years had well supplied;
Till she acquired sufficient skill,
Herself to teach, if she should will.

Examinations she had passed,
And had certificate at last;
And her ambition was to teach,
When this condition she should reach.

Her parents though could not agree,
That she should leave the family tree,
To brave the trials oft profound,
In such exacting service found.

But Agnes fain would put to test
The powers of which she felt possessed;

She would not be mere ornament,
E'en by her parents fond consent.

And so it came about one day,
The Principal had called to say,
That his Assistant had resigned,
And he must quick another find.

"I come to you," he said, " to ask
That you at once accept the task."

Miss Agnes sought and gained consent;
For here at home could well be spent
Her leisure hours with parents dear.
She took the place but with some fear,
Lest here among her neighbors she
Might not to this task equal be.

But soon her native talent rose
To match the duties which she chose;
And soon the Board, with one consent,
Would make position permanent.

Attention thus was drawn to her,
From watchful School Commissioner.

But when the term drew near its close
A strange and sad event arose:
One day her mother, Mrs. Daire,
Had fallen down the cellar stair,
And thus sustained an injury,
The end of which none could foresee.

To Agnes now was duty plain,
At home she surely would remain;
And with a daughter's filial love,
Supreme all other tasks above,
Would take her place as best she could,
And make return as daughter should,
For mother's love, and mother's care,
Through childhood's ills with patience rare.

When school was opened in the fall,
To the regret of children all,

A new assistant had arrived,
Instead of Agnes, so much loved.

With skillful treatment and with care,
Was rally quick with Mrs. Daire;
And so it chanced that Agnes found
Development for love profound,
Of music, which from childhood days
Had been a passion in some ways.

With small encouragement or aid,
Such aptitude had she displayed,
That long before her chubby hand
Had first the ivory octave spanned,
She played the melodies with skill,
Which her quick ear had caught at will.

She soon with "lessons" was employed,
And e'en the practice she enjoyed
For hours on each succeeding day,
When duties would afford the way;

And be it to her credit said,
She ne'er refused to give her aid,
At home, at school, at house of prayer,
In Sunday-school, or anywhere
That she could be of service true,—
Such instances, alas! are few.

She now had reached her eighteenth year,
Was tall and stately and sincere,
Had clear brown eyes that sparkled bright,
Or flashed disfavor at the sight
Of what was mean, or low, or vile;
Or kindled with approving smile,
At what was good, and pure, and clean;
Till none could doubt her choice between.

In feature she was strong and ripe,
Somewhat resembling Grecian type;
By nature of such gracious mind,
That she was uniformly kind;
Where merit she could plainly see
That was her chosen company.

AGNES DAIRE.

And such were her adorments rare
That she with grace her part could bear
At organ, or piano forte,
On croquet ground, or tennis court;
Could paint a picture, sing, recite,
Or creditable essay write;
Or in the kitchen take her place,
And there preside with equal grace;
Or spread a table at command,
With products of her own deft hand.

VI.

Walks and Talks.

The Better Part.

BRIGHT sun, in thy diurnal round,
    The haunts of men thou seest afar;
Which with the arts of peace resound,
    Or direful war.

Fair moon, thy dreamy brightness lures
    Fond lovers forth into the night;
Thy look emboldens, and assures
    The bashful wight.

Pale stars, ye gaze upon the deeds
    Of those who bend to sin's hard yoke;
Whose half reluctant courage needs
    Night's sable cloak.

All-seeing eye, alike to thee,
    Is night or day. O teach my heart
The bad to shun, and early see
    The Better Part.

VI. Walks and Talks.

SMALL wonder 'tis that ere they knew,
    Esteem 'twixt Joe and Agnes grew.

Like goodly service they performed,
To like good usages conformed.

And often when the Sunday-school
Would follow customary rule,
And hold a concert, or a drill,
These would their usual tasks fulfil:
Joe would to management give heed,
And Agnes at the organ lead;
And thus it often came about,
That when the exercise was out,
And little odds and ends were done,
These two would find them quite alone;
And so, of course, it was but right,
That Joe should act the gallant knight.

And soon the wise ones shook their head,
And winking to each other said:
"That's settled, you may be assured,"—
So food for gossip was secured.

And strange it is that to these twain,
What to less active minds was plain,
Was never e'en suspected true,—
The same old story, ever new!

Of mutual interests they would talk,
As slowly homeward they would walk;
The "small talk" of the town discuss;
Their tastes compare, their minds express;
But what was uppermost in each,
Had not the courage quite to reach.

But if suggestion had been made,
That they with love were ever swayed,
A stout denial had been met,—
And such delusions flourish yet!

"I have a notion," he expressed,
"That if I ever should be blessed
 With home and wife, her name might be
 The earnest of her love to me."

"Do you imply," said she, "or find,
 That names are omens of the mind?"

"Most surely I would have it so;
 Good names, good friends," said gallant Joe.

"But," she inquired, "How is it then
 That names so far precede the men?"

"You will admit," he kindly said,
"That in the Scripture may be read,
 That names and characters agree,
 Of all the worthies there you see."

"Your proof I challenge," she replied,
 Though half won over to his side.

THE HERMIT OF MOSS POND.

"Was Job not 'persecuted' sore?
 And Daniel 'judge' the people o'er?
 And Jacob, did he not 'supplant'?
 And Peter, firm as 'adamant'?"

"Ah yes. But still," she next inquired,
 Were not these Bible names inspired?"

"Inspired, indeed," he said, "but yet
 The natures did the names offset."

"But has not inspiration ceased?"
 Said Agnes, as the theme increased,
"Can parents now with certainty
 The future of their child foresee,
 And match the temper of the mind
 With name well suited to the kind?"

"Perhaps not always," Joe replied,
"And yet the rule may safely guide.
 Is not hereditary trait
 Quite sure to reappear, though late?

And if the tainted blood bear fruit,
In evils we may not compute;
Why may we not expect the pure
To have good fruitage quite as sure?
And would it not be safe to say,
As early as the christening day,
That those with lineage avowed,
Well born, well nurtured, well endowed,
Will not their heritage disclaim,
If this we certify by name?"

She listened with an interest deep,
Which to herself she could not keep.

Assured, he ventured to proceed,
"If to the altar I should lead
On some sweet day a charming bride,
'Twould be my all absorbing pride,
Whate'er might be the cherished name
Which at the altar she disclaim,
The one unchanged might be embraced
In classic garb as, Agnes—'chaste.'"

Had it been light Joe would have seen
Her cheek up-glow with crimson sheen;

But in the most indifferent way,
She said; "Perhaps it will, some day."

The homeward journey neared the end,
No further could this talk extend.

Now Joe sometimes had been impressed,
That he his calling had not guessed;
He had opinions well defined,
Was of religious turn of mind;
His duty was inclined to do,
When once that duty he well knew.

He had a good position now,
But was not easy quite somehow;
Should he not fit himself to preach,
And thus his proper calling reach?
And so this question in some shape,
His cautious lips would oft escape;

He longed to know but dared not ask,
What Agnes thought of such a task.

"Suppose I had a friend," he said,
"Who was in doubt where duty led;
 To whatsoe'er he turned his hand,
 It would not quite his mind command;
 But heard with every plan unfurled,
' Go preach my gospel to the world'?"

Joe put this question with some doubt,
But quick her answer came about:

" I would regard it as a call
 From grace divine, surmounting all."

" But how could he conclusion reach,
 That he was surely called to preach?"

" Perhaps 'twere better," she replied,
" If he another issue tried:

How could he ever be excused,
If such commission he refused?
It surely ought to be confessed,
That what endowments are possessed,
Should in the Master's service find
Employment suited to our mind;
If now your friend is well endowed,
Which by your question is allowed,
He ought to seek a service call,
Which would command his talents all."

"But may not one as useful be
  In other callings?" questioned he.

"Useful indeed," responded she,
"But not *as* useful, as you see.
  For nowhere else in this domain,
  Can godly talent hope to gain
 ⋅ Such grand results for labor done,
  As in the Gospel of God's Son.

For when the Savior would commend
The loving service of his friend,
He highest praise to mortals paid:
' She hath done what *she could*,' he said.

If one *can* preach the gospel pure,
'Tis highest duty, I am sure."

Joe winced a little as he heard,
For even so it had occurred
To his own conscientious mind;
But how to act he did not find.

" But if," said Joe, " my friend should be,
Toward gentler sex not quite heart free:
But felt a passion in his breast,
Which not as yet had been expressed;
Would not this also be a voice
Which would affect his final choice?"

" God's purposes are not thus mixed,"
   She said. " We need not choose betwixt

THE HERMIT OF MOSS POND.

The good and good, all one these twain;
For if 'tis true that Heaven ordain
A love for souls of sinful men,
And love which answers love again,
'Twere safe to follow Heaven's call,
And confidently venture all;
For highest human love is found
In hearts, if love of God abound."

Small comfort Joe received from this;
Yet, ere he could the thought dismiss,
Once more he ventured to inquire:
"What if this once expressed desire
Should haply in the sequel prove
To be a barrier to his love?"

This last did Agnes sorely vex,
As though indictment of her sex;
She thought a moment then replied;
"If mine 'twere ever to decide
Where love to God and duty plain
Would e'er conflict with selfish gain,

Whate'er would come my love between
I'd spurn it as a thing unclean."

And all unconscious of the pain
Had Agnes drawn his picture plain;
And as he left her at the gate,
Where just a moment he would wait,
He pressed her hand, and with a sigh,
"Suppose," he said, "that friend were I?"

The Christmas season now approached,
The festal subject had been broached.
According to time honored rule,
It was discussed in Sunday-school;
Committees were appointed, too,
And so the work in interest grew.
The Christmas tree must bear rich fruit,
Of various kinds each taste to suit,
And music must be practiced o'er,
And recitations, and much more.

So nightly Joe and Agnes met,
And held sweet converse, cherished yet;
Sometimes agreed on current uews;
Sometimes they differed in their views;
Though both to argue were inclined,
They always tried the truth to find;
These Christmas duties kept them late,
They oft were weary with their weight.

"I ne'er could see the reason why,"
Said Agnes, with a conscious sigh,
"That education is so planned,
As to ignore God's great command:
'Train up a child in wisdom's way,
And when he's old he will not stray.'"

The purport of this statement queer,
At first to Joe was not quite clear.

"What plan," he said, "would you approve,
Which your objection would remove?"

"I would encourage," she replied,
"If not demand, that it be tried,
  To teach the heart as well as head,
  When teachers by the state are paid.
  We tax ourselves to self protect,
  And then to best results object."

"Would you combine," said he, "in school,
  The teaching of the Golden Rule,
  With mathematics and the rest?"

  Joe said this only in a jest,
  But Agnes took him at his word.
"Indeed," she said, "what more absurd,
  Than for the state to school the mind,
  And leave the morals unrefined?
  And what the good to teach the law
  Of duties man to man may owe,
  But never once his debts review,
  Which to his God no less are due?"

"How far," said he, "would this extend,
If you should present laws amend?
Would not religion find its way
Into our public schools some day?"

She caught at this with eagerness;
"Religion, truly," said she, "yes,
Not false religion, but the true;
Just think a moment what we do;
We teach the system of the Greek,
And Homer's language learn to speak;
We hob-nob with the Roman gods,
As one through Virgil's measures plods;
Confucius too we study out,
For what the Chinese are about;
With bloody Turk,—Mohammedan,—
We con the stupid Alcoran;
And no one rises to object,
If Book of Mormon we inspect;
But, oh! ye gods of Greece and Rome,
And all the saints abroad or home!

The schools would evil breed instead,
If once the Bible should be read!
To teach religion is all right,
If once the true is not in sight!"

Joe listened with an interest real,
Which somehow he could scarce conceal;
And lured her on by skillful tact,
This fruitful subject to protract;
And though at times he felt the thrust,
Of lancet keen, sarcastic, just,
He thought his armor could afford
To yield to such a kindly sword.

"But is it not our policy,
  To educate the youth," said he,
"And leave religion to the church,
  Where those may freely find who search?"

"It yet remains," she said, " to prove
  That education will remove

Our ills, or in itself protect;
To that conclusion I object."

"But surely you would not maintain,"
Said Joe, to some advantage gain,
"That no protection we receive,
For all the money which we give?"

Her bright eyes flashed, her fair cheeks flamed,
At this delusive fiction named.

"Protection, yes, indeed," she said,
"I'll tell you how we are misled:
First, all the people by one rule
Are rightly taxed for public school;
Next, Christian people once more pay,
For church and Sunday-school outlay;
And at their own expense provide
The half the state leaves unsupplied.
For well they know that learned head,
With untamed heart we doubly dread;

And so, unselfish and devout,
They work to bring good ends about;
And even do not thus confine
Their gracious efforts to their own;
But with unselfish Christian zeal,
They labor for the public weal;
And so it happens that the state
Secures protection at that rate.

And even more, some would be glad
Insult to injury to add,
And tax these last the third time round,
For all the churches that abound."

" But would it do," he asked at length,
 That he might give his question strength,
" To tax the populace entire,
 For what but part of them desire?"

" Well said, if true," she answered quick,
" The state regards it politic

To educate the youth entire,
No matter what they may desire.

And is it not a patent truth,
That many thousands of these youth,
Among the lower strata found,
Where vice and crime and filth abound,
Themselves resist the proffered aid,
Content with idleness instead?
And so at school, by force, begin
The rudiments of discipline?"

"Quite true," said Joe, " I must agree;
But yet I do not clearly see,
How force could be resorted to,
To teach the Christian faith. Do you?"

"Not that, indeed," she said, "but yet,
Why not have liberty to get
A knowledge of that faith the same
As those called by less honored name?

WALKS AND TALKS.

The time will come, I do believe,
When men no longer can deceive;
When Christian sons of Christian sires
Will kindle patriotic fires
On every hilltop, and once more
Contend for freedom as of yore;
For are we not a Christian state?
Then why should we our faith abate?

If infidels and sceptics find
Our state too narrow for their mind,
Then let them migrate to some zone
Where God and Bibles are unknown.

To me it seems supremely strange,
That just a few can so arrange,
That what themselves have once decried,
Must be by law to all denied."

" But is it not quite true," said he,
" That good men, Christians, too, agree,

That state and church should be apart,
And head be not confused with heart?"

"Half true," she said, "but not believed.
No infidel has e'er received
The nation's honors as its chief;
Each ruler must express belief
In God, the ruler of the world;
And on his word, to him unfurled,
Pledge loyal service to his peers,
The while their honors he thus wears.

And juries, too, and witnesses,
In courts of justice must express
Belief in God and own his sway,
Ere they for service qualify.
And legislators, great and small,
And orators, and authors all,
When they would rise to lofty flights
Of eloquence o'er human rights,
Will quote the Bible rule supreme,
For argument to prove their theme.

And yet in public school, forsooth!
The Bible is denied the youth,
And would they dig in this rich mine,
For gems their speech to well refine;
They must with patience always wait,
Till through the schools kept by the state."

"What would you recommend?" said he.
"Just simply this," responded she,
"I'd make the Bible the first rule,
In every home, in every school;
And give it equal place among
The classic studies old or young;
Not force it out, nor force it in,—
Just give it chance its way to win."

"But in unworthy hands," said he,
"Would not there then some danger be?"

"Unworthy hands!" said she, polite,
"Would you the teachers thus indict?

'Some danger,' think you could result,
If God's own word we should consult?
With profit might we not compare
The Bible worthies with some care,
With 'Plutarch's Lives,' of classic fame,
And over-match them name for name?"

Now Agnes did not quite intend,
Thus far her strictures to extend;
Herself a teacher, much she saw
To well commend the present law;
Regretting only its defect
Which time, she hoped, would soon correct.

'Twas her ambition soon to see
The schools on this good plan agree:
To give the body exercise,
To train the mind till it is wise,
The morals also to amend,
Esthetic culture to extend,
The patriotic to inspire,
And let religion rule entire.

These all, in just proportions wrought,
Is learning to perfection brought.

"Of course, it matters not," said she,
With well intentioned irony,
"What I may think, or say, or do,—
For women have no vote, you know."

Howe'er, it is not out of place
To here remark, if by your grace,
If then Joe had been called to state
His verdict on that night's debate,
It surely would recorded be:
"For Agnes, one majority."

At last the Christmas eve approached,
Which on their time so much encroached.

One practice meeting yet remained,
And then the end would be attained;
The Christmas tree its fruit would bear,
And joy would reign without compare.

For Joe one thing remained, howe'er,
To make complete that Christmas cheer;
One gift all other gifts above,
He most desired: 'Twas Agnes' love.
But could he hope the prize to gain?
Or, would he plead his cause in vain?

A thousand plans he formed amiss,
At last he settled down to this.

That very night he would declare
His ardent love for Agnes Daire,
Would write a letter, and inclose
A diamond ring, and this propose:
That if his love she could receive,
She wear the ring on Christmas eve.

Once formed, this purpose filled his mind.
The ring was purchased, note outlined
And copied o'er and o'er with care,—
Nought was too good for Agnes Daire.

WALKS AND TALKS.

All through the day and evening, too,
It burned almost his pocket through;
He thought his looks almost revealed,
What mind and pocket thus concealed.

The evening came to end at last,
The homeward journey soon was passed;
And strangely, too, for scarce a word
By either was expressed or heard;
But both were busied with the thought
Which soon was to an issue brought.

For Joe's queer silence we have key,
If explanation there need be;
And Agnes was not so obtuse,
That she had failed to find excuse.

When Joe had said his last good night,
He gave her hand a pressure slight,
And placed the precious note therein,
With gift designed her love to win.

Grown somewhat bolder, after this
He printed on her hand a kiss.

The time for parting now had come,
He walked on air his journey home.

VII.
Defalcation.

Misunderstood.
Rondeau.

MISUNDERSTOOD! a life undone,
  Ere half th' allotted race is run.
    'Tis ever thus;—we mourn, we cry
    O'er fancied wrongs, and oft deny
  Sweet Peace approach, till hope is gone.

  Or if, perchance, we struggle on,
  And bear life's ills as best we can,
    Oft 'neath the burden must we sigh,—
      Misunderstood.

  Faint not, dear heart, nor duty shun;
  Through sacrifice of self, God's Son
    Redeemed a world; should not we try
    To act our part, and magnify
  Our Lord, e'en though by all save one,
      Misunderstood?

VII. Defalcation.

EXCITEMENT held the little town,
  That Christmas day, and henceforth on;
The station agent oft was plied
With questions he could not decide;
The business seemed all in share;
No clue as yet had found escape;
The books were posted neat and true;
The tickets ran their numbers through;
In short no reason could be traced,
Why Joe departed in such haste;
And so the gossip rose and fell,
Till every burgher knew it well;
But none so wise as to foresee,
What might the final issue be.

The old year waned, the new at hand,
Must take the records as they stand;
The agent sent in his report,
For balance of the season short,

Since that eventful day when Joe
Had disappeared from public view.

On New Year's day a stranger guest
Made his appearance at Green Crest.—
A high official,—Mr. Howe,
Whose nephew was the agent now.

An air of mystery he wore,
The while he conned the records o'er.

He and the agent worked all day,
From early morn till evening gray,
And oft were seen to shake the head,
But of their business nothing said.

When Mr. Howe left town that night,
The records proved to be all right;
But funds, according to report,
Were seven hundred dollars short.

DEFALCATION.

The story ran from mouth to mouth,
To north, and east, and west, and south,
Till all the town was nearly wild,
O'er what had been that day revealed.

"Defaulter!" was on every tongue;
And "fugitive," were changes rung;
Till wearied by the exercise,
They waited for some new surprise.

At last the secret had come out,
Joe Manly was a thief, no doubt!

To Agnes came this awful news,
Like killing frost on summer dews.
The flowers which sprang up in her heart,
That gladsome time they last did part,
Lay chilled and withered by the blight,
And even hateful to her sight.

That dreadful night she tried to pray,
Which had her refuge been alway;

But form of words she could not find,
Except there crowded in her mind,
The Psalmist's faith in dire distress,
And thus her soul she did express:

"If I in trouble do abide,
In his pavilion he will hide;
He'll keep me safe and secret, too,
If enemies my soul pursue."

A firm resolve she formed that night,
That she would be consistent quite;
Faith was her duty, not more plain
In sunshine than in chilling rain.
"I will believe of doubt instead,
Help thou mine unbelief," she said.

Some keen detectives now begun
To ferret out the guilty one;
But disappointment they endured,
For not a clue could be secured.

DEFALCATION.

For Joe had not his plans revealed,
Nor on the other hand concealed;
And for the very good excuse,
He had no plan yet formed for use.

A letter was indeed received,
Requesting that he be relieved
From his entire relation now,
For reasons he could not avow.
But thought no one at all concerned,
If his location were not learned.

The envelope showed no imprint,
Save " D. & H. IN TRANSIT," sent;
Which is the case with transient mail,
Thus locally sent o'er the rail.

And so the matter must be dropped,
Until some circumstance outcropped,
To put the officers on track,
Or Joe himself, perchance, came back.

VIII.
Some Letters.

December and June.

How short, and dark, and cold, in icy winter's garb,
Are days whose southern and low-circling orb
   Slants to the earth his dim, reluctant ray.
   But when in summer time, treading his northward way,
The sun makes haste to rise, or lingers to depart,
For joy at song of birds, or busy hum of mart,
   While flowe's and babbling brooks make glad his stay,
   Ere full aware his tardiness prolongs the day.

VIII. Some Letters.

THESE chronicles must now return,
Some previous events to learn.

About a league, toward the west
Along the railway, from Green Crest,
A hamlet lay amid the hills.
Its industry of knitting mills
Employment to the people gave,
And income both to use and save.

The people prospered as a rule,
And well sustained their village school.
Good teachers only were employed,
Good wages were by them enjoyed,
And when a change sometimes occurred,
Widespread regret was often heard.
And such a change was now at hand,
Which our attention must command;
Because to small extent at least,
By this was Joe's distress increased.

THE HERMIT OF MOSS POND.

The teacher at Glenvale was ill,
And her position could not fill.
She struggled bravely through the term,
But toward the end was so infirm,
That it was plain she must decide,
To sure resign at Christmas tide.

The school trustee at once set out
To bring the needed change about.
He thought it wise to first confer
With trusty School Commissioner.

The case was stated with some strength,
And so it came about, at length,
That Joseph Price, the school trustee,
Received this answer to his plea:

Dear sir:
        In answer to your note
This day received, I gladly quote
A list of teachers well endowed,
Of whom I am quite justly proud;

And at the head without compare,
I place the name of Agnes Daire.
With kind regards,
>	I am, dear sir,
Yours truly,
>	Stern,
>	>	Commissioner.

Without delay he sent this note
To Agnes Daire, which here we quote:

Miss Agnes Daire,
>	From Mr. Stern,
Our School Commissioner, I learn
Your name, and by his kind advice,
I write to offer liberal price,
If you consent the place to fill
Of teacher who has fallen ill.
If you accept I will consent
To wait till Holidays are spent;
And at your leisure I will call
To close a contract, and withal

Consult what plans we may express,
For your convenience and success.
With much respect, till you I see,
Yours truly,
>   Joseph Price,
>   Trustee.

' Twas on December twenty third,
That this transaction had occurred.

As Henry Daire came from his store,
When labors of the day were o'er,
He brought this letter, just arrived
By evening mail, and so contrived
How it might reach his daughter's sight,
When she arrived from church that night.

For Agnes, we already know,
That night did to the practice go.

Upon her table by her bed,
Had Mr. Daire the letter laid;

SOME LETTERS.

And there 'twas found, as he had planned,
And, ere she slept, by Agnes scanned.

Unhappy Agnes! that thine eye
Could not have passed that letter by!

With Joe's warm kiss upon her hand,
With courage she could scarce command,
Had Agnes hastened to her room,
That at the issue she might come.

She broke the seal, the diamond bright
First met her joy bedizzened sight;
And next she read Joe's message through,
Which now is here transcribed anew:

Dear Agnes,
         If I may lay claim,
To call thee by that precious name;
Accept this token of my love,
All earthly passions else above.

And if I may the hope indulge,
Of love returned, that boon divulge,
By wearing on thy cherished hand,
This gem-surmounted golden band;
And every flashing ray of light
Shall be my answer and delight.
But if,—my pen would fain decline
To write the portents of this line,—
But if thy heart can find no place
For my poor love, ah! then efface
My image from thy heart, and thrust
This bauble to its kindred dust.
But till thy answer I obtain,
I feast on hope, and so remain,
As ever, thine through weal or woe,
Your faithful, hopeful servant,

                    JOE.

Her cup ran o'er; such happiness
She did not know, or even guess,
Could come to mortals here below.
And then her thoughts went out to Joe.

"Poor Joe," she said, "you shall not wait
The whole day through, and night, till late,
To have your answer; I will write
Before I sleep, this very night."

As joy we double, grief divide,
By sharing with a comrade tried,
She was not quite supremely blest,
With this sweet secret in her breast.
She read the letter, o'er and o'er,
For surely twenty times or more;
She watched the diamond's chromic gleam,
To be assured she did not dream;
Then on her finger placed the ring,
Which should to Joe assurance bring.

Now when the night was well nigh spent,
Her wearied energies were bent,
To make reply to both these notes,
Which this above narration quotes;
Then crept into her bed, at last,
Where sleep profound soon held her fast.

The hour was late, next morn, before
The servant rapped at Agnes' door;
No answer came,—she entered then,
And took the situation in.

There Agnes lay in sweet repose,
Her cheeks were crimson as a rose,
A smile, as if of peace, o'erspread
Her face, and haloed her fair head.
One hand lay there in vision plain,
Uncovered on the counterpane;
And on her finger sparkled bright,
The diamond placed there yesternight.

The servant was a maid herself;
Was proud, though not possessed of pelf,
And served for wages, when her state
Was with her pride commensurate.
She had the weakness of her sex,
For jewels and such charms complex;
And when she saw the diamond rest
On Agnes' finger, quickly guessed

Its full portent, and stood enwrapped,
By curiosity entrapped.

Ah, yes! and she is not the first,
Who by their dire abnormal thirst
For news to which they have no right,
Involved their neighbors in sad plight.

She looked about the room straightway;
There on the table letters lay,
Addressed and stamped but yet unsealed.

A look at Agnes quick revealed,
That she was held by sleep profound;
Then glancing quickly all around,
She took the letters from their shield,
And soon devoured the secrets held.

When these as quickly were replaced,
She left the room with guilty haste;
One moment paused outside the door,
Then rapped more loudly than before.

Now Agnes was aroused at last,
A puzzled look about her cast,
Tried to recall her scattered sense,
And verify last night's events;
" Had she been dreaming all this joy?"
" Was waking only to annoy?"

She tried to make her senses act.
The jeweled finger was a fact;
There lay the letters on the stand,
The product of her own free hand.

She bade the servant enter now,
And her excuses did avow,
For over-sleeping in such style;
And quickly robed herself meanwhile.

And when she saw the hour was late,
That postman now was at the gate,
She sealed the letters, quick as thought,
And bade the maid to hand them out.

As soon as breakfast was well o'er,
Her mother shared her heart's fond store
Of joy and hope, not loth to tell.
She answered: "Darling, it is well,"
And kissed her fondly, and embraced,
" 'Tis well my daughter, Agnes, 'chaste.' "

And, at the noon time, Henry Daire
Was of this secret made aware;
And he, too, blessed his darling child,
And tearfully approval smiled.

Unhappy, happy Agnes, thou!
Joy on, while yet you may, for now,
Yes even now, the lightning stroke,
O'er thy devoted head has broke,
For smiles are tears, for joy is pain,
When will there sunshine be again?

The strange events which on that day,
We have before tried to portray,

May from this letter now be guessed,
Which had so sorely Joe distressed:

Dear Sir:—

Your favor of this date,
I haste to answer; and to state
That with regret I must decline
To entertain your offer fine;
My parents, too, resist the thought,
Of sacrifice so dearly bought;
My thanks howe'er must be expressed,
For favor of such kind request;
Howe'er unwelcome this reply,
' *Tis final* as you must rely.
With much respect, I am, dear sir,
Yours very truly,

          Agnes Daire.

One letter yet remains to trace,
Which had that morning left the place:

As Joseph Price, on Christmas eve,
Came home from church, he did receive
A letter postmarked from Green Crest.

It reached Glenvale by last mail west,
And when he was ensconced at home,
In his somewhat unsocial room,
He dressed him in his reading gown,
And with composure settled down,
To read the letter at his ease,
And learn the issue,—if it please.

Now Joseph was a bachelor,
A veteran of the civil war,
His shoulder straps he bravely won
As captain ere the war was done;
A widowed mother kept his home,
Since from the army he had come;
Was popular in all Glenvale,
With young and old, infirm or hale;
Was "fat and forty," sleek of dress,
And well preserved, and had access

To all the "functions" of the town,
Social or civic in renown.

He had been school trustee for years,
And was a leader 'mong his peers;
Polite and affable and kind,
And of a social turn of mind;
And though his years ran on apace,
He had a youngster's heart and face.

Tonight he was quite ill at ease;
For at the church, on Christmas trees,
He had received such gifts, in size
And value, as to quite surprise:

Three pairs of slippers, worked by hand,
With patient skill, in pattern grand;
A reading cap, embroidered o'er;
And Christmas cards, full half a score.

What did it mean, he asked himself,
As these lay marshalled on his shelf.

Ah me! at last he sighed, in vain,
" I wish I were quite young again."

Now to his task he settled down,
And soon relapsed to " study brown."

" Dear Joe,"—" Well, well, the little minx!
I really wonder what she thinks?"

" Dear Joe,—
   The proffered prize I take,"
" There, now, I can some headway make.
She will accept the school to teach,
To that conclusion I can reach."

" Dear Joe," he read again.—" Let's see,
A little queer, to thus call me;
But then these girls are full of pranks,—
A bonnie lass this girl of Hank's."

Now Joseph Price and Henry Daire,
Had once been playmates and friends rare,

And so we may the custom thank,
That they were known as "Joe," and "Hank."
Hence Captain Price, perhaps might know,
Why he should be addressed as Joe,
But why it should be written "dear,"
That surely seemed a little queer.

If "Mr. Joe," or "Captain Joe,"
Or "Trustee Joe," then that would go;
But then, at last, he figured out,
It might have this way come about:

"Now Hank himself the letter writ
For Agnes, that's the way of it."

"Or else," said he, "I am not old,
Just forty, if the truth is told,
Well settled in a cozy home,
Who knows what may be the outcome?

The daughter of my dear old friend,
Might possibly such answer send.

SOME LETTERS.

Let's see, what did I write to her,
I have forgotten, I aver.
Is that word *prize*, or *price*, she makes?
Suppose the 'proffered *Price* she takes.'
I don't believe I clearly see,
If she accepts the *school*, or *me*!"

Then in his desk he fished around,
And some old scraps of paper found,
On which in part the draft appeared,
Of his own letter scratched and bleared.

" I do declare!" he said at length,
With muster of his trembling strength,
I fear instead of wages pelf,
I just have offered her myself.
I'd give my eyes, if I could see,
If that was writ a capital P.
For here it stands, as cold as ice,
' *I write to offer liberal price!* '."

Nor were it strange, if it occurred
In writing such familiar word
As one's own name, that such mistake
Might easily a fellow make.

Well, what a mix, but let it go;
Whiche'er it is, it shall be so,
And never to my latest day,
Shall anybody rise to say,
That through a blunder of his life,
Joe Price obtained a charming wife."

He put the letter safe away,
To be reviewed some other day;
And meanwhile planned to make believe,
That Agnes would the school receive.

Here is the letter, as it stands,
Which our attention now commands:

Dear Joe,

    The proffered prize I take,
And wear it gladly for your sake;
But beg you not to overrate
My modest worth or humble state;
But what of love my heart contains,
All undivided yours remains;
And happy shall I ever be,
To write,
    Yours truly,
        Agnes D.

IX.

Decline.

If Anything Happens.

—Rondeau.—

"IF ANYTHING happens," wherever I rove,
On land or on ocean, in temple or grove,
Defending home altars in liberty's cause,
Or peacefully heeding humanity's laws,—
My soul will fly hither, on wings of the dove.

Through duty and danger triumphant I'll move,
And brief our adieux in the language of love —
   A volume of meaning condensed in a clause,—
     " If anything happens."

So out from thy presence, where duties behoove,
I go but my heartfelt devotion to prove ;
   A wealth of success if I win thy applause,
   But if—ah! the thought makes my life current pause,—
Remember me kindly, and meet me above,
     " If anything happens."

IX. Decline.

'TWAS rather late that Christmas eve,
When Agnes for the church did leave.

The happy hours from morn to night,
Were counted off with glad delight,
Much as a faithful devotee
Counts beads upon a rosary.

And when the time for service came,
She tripped away with heart aflame.

She noticed when she reached the church,
That she was eyed with curious search.

Her entrance caused a mild surprise,
But what it meant did not surmise.

But when she climbed the organ stair,
She saw Joe Manly was not there.

But no one had vouchsafed to tell
The wondering Agnes what befell;
And so she was quite unaware,
Until she heard the closing prayer,
And then her joy was turned to woe,
The " Wanderer " was surely Joe.

Her father met her in the aisle,
And tried her anguish to beguile;
He, too, had heard the rumor wild,
And hastened to protect his child;
Convoyed her home and gently told
What of the case he could unfold.

What happened there for days and days,
Is rightly hidden from our gaze;
That Joe had disappeared was plain,
But why, she could not ascertain;
Till on that fatal New Year's day,
The story spread to her dismay,
That Joe was wrong in his accounts,
And had defaulted large amounts.

Did she believe it? Surely no,
What woman would have failed him so?

"If he is innocent," she said,
"He'll need a friend, of foes instead;
If he has fallen,—God forbid!—
E'en though his fault may not be hid,
He needs a friend, 'tis plain to see,
And shall have friends in God and me."

Oh faithful woman, and sublime!
What would the world, with all its crime,
Mistakes, and weakness, ever do,
If thou, perchance, shouldst prove untrue?

"There must be some mistake," she said,
Then o'er and o'er Joe's letter read;
"For one who could such message write,
Did sure not feel his conscience smite."

Soon after New Year's day was past,
She was in deeper trouble cast.

For Joseph Price, the school trustee,
About the contract called to see.

Prepared he was for any fate,—
Whichever way the case relate.

At first he halted at the store,
To talk their old acquaintance o'er;
Then made his way to Mrs. Daire,
To wisely seek for favor there;
And there was shocked to be replied,
That Agnes was to guests denied.

" 'Tis very urgent," he had said,
Then showed the letter to be read.

To Agnes now her mother went,
To learn the letter's strange intent.

Poor Agnes took the fatal dart,
And pressed it sadly to her heart.

"This letter which was meant for Joe,
To Joseph Price did surely go;
And that for Captain Price designed,
Its way to Joe as surely find;
And so, alas! it must be plain,
That Joe was driven away in pain."

And as her eye ran o'er the note,
She slightly changed it as we quote:
"*Dear Joe, the proffered prize I take,
And wear it, though my heart may break.*"

Now such a man was Joseph Price,
That, when acquainted with the case,
Assured his friends of service best,
And hid their secret in his breast.

The weary winter dragged its length,
And so declined poor Agnes' strength.

The spring and summer filed along,
And found her daily still less strong,

Till her physician ordered change,—
Such brooding might her mind derange.

Now Agnes blamed herself alway,
For the mistake of that sad day;
Until the conscience stricken maid,
Had on herself the mischief laid;
And had the circumstance confessed,
Which act had Agnes so distressed:

"I read the letters, and in haste,
Perhaps, I changed them when replaced."

But though the truth some comfort gave,
It came too late the wrong to save;
And so 'twas thought the safest rule,
To place her in some noted school;
And so employment suited find,
For her somewhat distracted mind.

X.

School.

The Chapel Bell.

—Sonnet.—

RING out, old bell! For years three score and ten,
   Since first thy voice awoke the echoing trills,
   Of Susquehanna's virgin wooded hills,
Thou'st called to learning's sacred halls, young men
And maidens fair, who since with tongue or pen,
   Or in such other sphere as heaven wills,
   Have blessed the world and modified its ills;—
Ring out, old bell, a welcome once again.
And when the angel trump that wakes the dead,
   And calls the faithful to the Master's rest,
     Shall sound o'er land and sea, at last, to tell
That time shall be no more, may we not dread
   Its summoning voice, but heed its glad behest,
     As we have answered to thy call, old bell.
1815—1885.

X. School.

WHEN once it was the settled rule,
That Agnes should be placed in school,
It somehow puzzled them to know,
Just where 'twas best for her to go.

The magazines they searched to find
The school announcements of this kind.
Then sent for catalogues and price,
That they might make desired choice.

But if they were at loss before,
They well might now be puzzled more;
For schools there were of every kind,
But few just suited to their mind.

Now Agnes needed home-like care,
That contrast might not be severe;
With work her mind to occupy,
And exercise to strength supply.

A year would be enough, they thought,
To make complete the learning sought;
And bring her mind to such a state,
As would become a graduate.

And so were catalogues perused,
For some advice which might be used.

One offered great facility
For boating contests, and such glee;
And this year stood an even chance,
To gain renown, and so advance
To first rank in fraternity,
By entry into "Varsity."

One had a champion foot-ball team,
Which brought the school to great esteem;
And such the valor of the men,
That in their sports time and again,
Had limbs been broken, noses split,—
Each would so well himself acquit.

And once, it was with boasting said,
One had been carried homeward dead.

Another would their students drill,
In contests of athletic skill;
And had a record of this sort,—
The envy of the student sport:
In running jump of height six feet,
One had a score that none could beat;
One put a twelve-pound shot away,
For three-and-forty feet one day;
And one could vault a fence with ease,
For seven feet, if so he please;
But crowning all, the school's great pet,
Could kick nine feet in air,—"you bet!"

In some, fraternities abound,
Of secret order quite profound;
And to distinguish their own "set,"
Had ravished the Greek alphabet;
And oft the "anti's" had averred,
When "scraps" with "frats" sometimes occurred,

That these symbolic letters few,
Were all the Greek the members knew.

And still another offered aid,
For training of another grade;
Here under tutors was a chance,
To learn the mazes of the dance;
The rules of etiquette were taught,
And so to great perfection brought;
The social was so emphasized,
That most of school life it comprised.

Some schools indeed it almost looks,
Paid small attention to their books;
And others seemed to have some "fad,"
Which chiefly their attention had.

In one 'twas *Physics*, and the room
Was one museum, we presume;
Or *Chemistry*, and so the space,
For bottles and retorts found place;

Or *Classics*, with attention shown
All languages except our own;
Or *military drill*, perhaps,
With tinsel lace and shoulder straps.

'Twould not be altogether good,
From these exhibits to conclude,
That all the schools are thus inclined;
But still too many such we find;
'Tis best, perhaps, to be advised
That *nostrums* are *most advertised*.

It soon was altogether plain,
That from this source they would not gain
The object of their eager search;
Then they remembered, once, at church,
Their pastor had with interest rare,
Commended to his people's care,
A Christian school, if need there be,
To send their children thus away.

" 'Tis well, my people," he had said,
" To guard the heart as well as head;
These godless schools may turn your child
From wisdom's way to customs wild;
For just at that susceptive age,
Some error may their thought engage;
And with no Christian teacher near,
Much mischief may be done, I fear."

And so they sought their pastor's aid,
And all arrangements with him made,
To thence convoy their daughter dear,
And see her settled for a year.

XI.
The Hermit.

Reclaimed.

—Sonnet.—

THE lordly pine which, from its dizzy height,
  Looks down o'er many a foot of unlimbed trunk,
  Was once a twig whose tiny branches shrunk,
And died, neglected in the upward flight,
Of the ambitious terminal toward light;
  The while these axillary buds were sunk,
  Beneath exogenous folds, ere they had drunk
The nectar brewed their growth to expedite.

Our lives, though in their origin possessed,
  Of embryo bud, or weakling branch of sin,
    May yet through Faith and Love be made to rise,
To glorious ungnarled height, which may be dressed
  Fit for the Heavenly Builder's use, within
    That house not made with hands, beyond the skies.

11. The Hermit.

'TIS now our duty to return,
And something of the wanderer learn.

Our paths, since parallel they run,
Must be traced singly since begun.

When Joe, on that sad Christmas day,
Awoke his strange lodge to survey;
No explanation could he find,
To satisfy his puzzled mind.
So when the sun descended low,
He thought he would to clearing go,
And learn before the night advance,
Somewhat of his retreat, perchance.

He took the trail by which he came,
Then saw the western sky aflame;
While at his feet in beauty lay,
The river with its winding way,—

A silver ribbon glazed with ice;
Then he discovered in a trice,
That on that yester-night his quest,
Was toward the east, instead of west.

Then he retracked the forest road,
And sought again last night's abode.

He thought he soon would leave the place,
His wandering pathway to retrace,
But could not quite decision form.

The cabin kept him fed and warm,
Till New Year's day had quickly passed,
And woodsmen had returned at last.

They were surprised when they did come,
To find a tenant thus at home;
But explanations were supplied,
Till all their doubts were satisfied;
And in their work Joe soon engaged,
And so his grief was some assuaged.

THE HERMIT.

It was agreed his wages went,
Entirely for the cabin rent;
And for such usage of supplies,
As would his scanty wants comprise.

And so congenial was it found,
That when the spring had come around,
And woodsmen had their task complete,
Joe held the use of this retreat.

So by degrees the story spread,
That near Moss Pond a Hermit dread,
Was dwelling in a cabin rude,
Within the mountain virgin wood.

But farthest was it from Joe's thought,
To such tradition to be brought.

The winter labor for him found
Some panacea for his wound,
And summer's rest gave ample time
For meditative thoughts sublime.

And every night he made a vow,—
If Heavenly Father would, somehow,
Bring order out of chaos dire,
Which held his soul almost entire,
His ransomed powers he would devote,
His righteous kingdom to promote.

XII.

Moss Pond.

October.

THY alternating smiles and tears, though not unlike the April showers,
   Fall round the graves instead of cradles, of the joy-inspiring flowers;
Thy somber hues look rearward, to the fruitful summer's ripened grain,
But forward to the killing frosts, and all their white-clad wintry train,
Thy sunset's golden glories, held imprisoned in the maple boughs,
   Bring grief or gladness as they hint of perfidy or plighted vows;—
For now the "season's" ended, and back homeward turns the human tide,
Whatever be the wooing, fair October claims a wintry bride.

XII. Moss Pond.

AMONG Otsego hills, is found
   A chain of lakes which cluster round
The Susquehanna River's head,
Like jewels which a crown o'erspread.

With one of these we have to do,
And that, one of the smallest, too;
Hid in surrounding forests deep,
As though in Nature's lap asleep.

Its name appropriate it bears,
From mossy kerchief which it wears;

For, round its curved periphery,
A margin of dense moss we see,
Which from the shore extends beyond,
Well toward the centre of the pond.

Or, if the mountain we compare
To monster lying outstretched there,

The pond would be cyclopean eye,
Steadfastly gazing toward the sky;
The iris is the mossy marge,
The open centre pupil, large.

So dense this curious mossy bed,
That one may safely on it tread,
E'en to the curving central bound,
Where sparkling water may be found.

The colors of this carpet strange,
All through the prismic spectrum range,
Of gold and russet, red and green,
Of gray, and brown, and silvery sheen;
With all the tints, and shades, and hues,
Which one in earth or sky e'er views.

Moreover with the changing year,
These colors also changed appear;
For in these mosses leaves entwine,
Of cranberries and aqueous vine,

MOSS POND.

Whose ripening fruit, and berries red,
Seem figures worked with beads instead.

Here one may stand, if so he please,
And "teeter" up and down with ease.
Till waves of carpet roll along,—
So dense the moss, and also strong.

And yet a cane will easy go,
Down through the moss to depths below.

The water of this lakelet queer,
Is found to be surprising clear;
And multitudes of cat-fish find
Conditions suited to their kind.

Moss Pond for years has been a shrine,
For those who to romance incline;—
For lovers fond and students gay,
Who wish to wile a summer day.

'Tis reached by trail which may be found,
To eastward of the Indian Mound;
Which curiosity, betimes,
Was elsewhere mentioned in these rhymes.

XIII.

Recognition and Explanation.

Resurgam.

—Sonnet.—

A MODEST flower in a garden grew,—
   The garden was of old well tilled and fair,
   The flower breathed its perfume on the air
As gentle breezes 'mong its petals blew.
Responsive to refreshing rain and dew,
   Oft bloomed this choice perennial, to bear
   Its meeds of joy to eye and mind, and wear
Its roseate crown of variagated hue.

When dearth appeared, the flower drooped—and died.
   Dead! Dead? vibrated on a thousand lips;
     A thousand eyes dropped tears. The tears were rain,
Which waked the slumbering sprite. The vital tide
   Reflowed, as life returns when nature sips
     The breath of spring. The flower bloomed again.

XIII. Recognition and Explanation.

WITH Agnes school life well agreed;
   Her mind from brooding had been freed,
By occupation which engaged
Her fertile thought, and grief assuaged.

The winter passed and spring arrived,
When busy students oft contrived
To find some relaxation meet,
To match their weariness complete;

For after long and tiresome work,
What wonder that they sometimes shirk,
When balmy spring invites to roam,
And languors of "Spring Fever" come.

One day in June—well nigh the end,—
Petition did the students send
The faculty, for holiday,
A visit to Moss Pond to pay.

To Hartwick Seminary folk,
'Tis quite a stale perennial joke;
For while all join in such request,
But few these projects interest.

Some want the day for shopping trip,
Some would the more their mind equip
For "Regents'" now quite near at hand,
And some the day in fishing spend.

One name will cover all:—Moss Pond,
Each has his reason this beyond.

But once at least should all incline,
To make a journey to this shrine.

This year howe'er, it came about,
That quite a party started out,
Of students, teachers, parents, too,
The interesting sights to view;
To have pic-nic outing rare,
And rest the mind from toilsome care.

As is the habit, in such case,
The youngsters with each other race;
And all the journey is thus done,
With flash of wit, and joke, and fun.

And one rash student e'en was found,
To roll the slope of Indian Mound;
But one such venture proved enough,
So steep the journey, and so rough.

The dainty lunch was much enjoyed,
Which for this purpose was convoyed;
And then for hours, as each thought best,
Was pleasure sought, or timely rest.

Some caught the catfish for the sport;
Some paid respects to Cupid's court;
Some ventured on the mossy bed;
Some otherwise, as fancy led;
And one,—and he Professor, too,
So bold and venturesome he grew,—

That on a temporary raft,
Would sail, while his companions laughed,
To see the antics he displayed,
As these brief voyages were made,
Till by a misdirected stroke,
Involuntary bath he took.

Now Agnes was herself inclined
Botanic specimens to find,
And sassafras, and wintergreen,
And orchids which may here be seen.

She wandered out alone some way,
And toward the north her journey lay;
Till out of her companions' sight,
Though of this fact unconscious quite.

She oft had heard the story told,
About the Moss Pond Hermit old;
But gave no heed as she would hear,
Nor thought it now worth while to fear.

With hat bedecked with running pine,
And dogwood flowers and columbine,
She heedless through the thicket pressed,
For trophies to reward her quest.

When she would now rejoin her friends,
And for her absence make amends,
To her amazement, in her way,
The Hermit stood, in garb of gray,
With bearded face and curious mien,
Such as before she had not seen.

She gave a piercing cry of fright,
When this strange vision met her sight;
She tried to run, but caught her feet,
In tangled vines of bittersweet;
And helpless lay, half dead with fear,
When she beheld the Hermit near.

" Fair lady," said he gallantly,
" You need not fear unworthy me.

Tell me your errand, whence you came,
Or whither you would go, just name,
And it will be my cheerful task
To guide you safe where'er you ask."

Could Agnes now believe her ears?
That voice so pleading calmed her fears;
It had a strange, familiar sound,
Which echoed in her soul profound.

She raised her hand to shield her eyes;
She tried to look in her surprise;
The diamond on her finger flashed;
The Hermit sorely was abashed.

Their glances met, they both cried out;
"Joe!" "Agnes!" "How came this about?"

"And are you then alive?" she said,
"My love has mourned you, as if dead."

"What! love?" he said, "your *love* has mourned?
How can that be, with my love scorned?"

"Scorned, Heaven forbid! See there," she said,
Then to his gaze her hand outspread.
"'And every flashing ray of light
Shall be my answer and delight.'
These are your words to me addressed,
And this the answer then expressed;
Poor Joe, misfortune 'twas not fault,
But let the end the means exalt,
Which gives us back to life our dead,
And yields us flowers of thorns instead."

"How is it then," he quick inquired,
"That this misfortune has occurred?
Here is the letter I received,
Which has my spirit sorely grieved."

"That letter was for Joseph Price,
Not Joseph Manly. By device

Of naughty servant it was sent
To you, instead of him I meant."

It clearly would not do to stay
Much longer from her friends away;
So while their souls o'erflowed their eyes
Did Agnes once again arise,
And give her jeweled hand to Joe,—
" Now to my comrades I must go."

It is not meet for curious eye,
Into this brief adieu to pry;
What plans were laid for future need,
Will be outlined as we proceed.

Joe guided Agnes on her way,
Till he must needs his journey stay;
She joined her friends, but not too soon,
For though the days are long in June,

The homeward march must be begun,
Forewarned by the descending sun.

And now a strange discussion rose:
Who could the mystery disclose?
What had occurred to Agnes Daire?
So fresh, so bright, so glad, so fair!
This maid so modest and so coy,
Was half beside herself with joy.

For this great change none could account,
" Was she transfigured on the mount?"

XIV.

Graduation.

The Diploma.

Rondeau.

LIKE flakes of snow, down failing fast,
    In bleak December's wintry blast,
  Now at the season's radiant noon,
  In rosy, gladsome month of June,
Descends a cloud white-winged and vast.

From *alma mater's* rich repast,
Are academic parchments cast,
  For their own season opportune,
    Like flakes of snow.

Some, like snow-crystals unsurpassed,
Bring matchless beauty, long to last;
  Some, too, forsooth are trodden soon,
  'Neath wanton feet, a slighted boon,
Unvalued and unheeded passed,
    Like flakes of snow.

XIV. Graduation.

THE summer term at Hartwick passed,
   With Agnes cheerful quite at last.

She wisely had indulged in sport,
Such as with dignity comport.

Her studies, too, she well pursued,
The new she learned, the old reviewed,
And passed the Regents' of that day,
Till academic honors lay
Within her reach as graduate.
It only now remained to state
By thesis her research mature,
And her Diploma thus secure.

Just here a difficulty lay;
For graduates too often pay
More heed to outward garb refined,
Than to adornments of the mind.

Some ladies of that graduate class
Their predecessors would surpass,
In rich display, and costly dress.
Now Agnes this did much distress.

By nature she was disinclined
To such debasement of the mind.

She plead for neat simplicity,
Which to her mind would more agree
With common sense and cultured taste,
Than such unnecessary waste.

Then, too, she could not quite consent,
To deck herself in gay ostent,
The while such rigors of distress,
Ofttimes her wounded soul possess.

Some members, too, could ill afford
To meet extravagance absurd;
And to their credit, be it told,
The class did Agnes' view uphold;

And so much labor and expense,
Has thus been spared from that day hence.

Commencement week was now at hand,
For which the class had long time planned.

The sermon baccalaureate
Had ushered in the yearly fete.

Then followed lectures, class-day sports,
Prize essays, annual reports,
Until the end was reached at last,
And final muster must be passed.

This Agnes had been dreading long;
Though well equipped she was not strong,
And sought seclusion in her state,
For reasons she could not relate;
And though her tasks were always done,
And prize for essay had been won,
About her was mysterious air,
Which none had fathomed, quite, thus far.

And more, all precedent beyond,
Since that strange pic-nic at Moss Pond;
For now instead of ways demure,
She seemed to dwell in sunlight pure.

Her parents came that evening late,
To see their daughter graduate.

They were surprised, delighted, too,
But of this change they nothing knew,
Nor guessed, but only feared the fact,
That this excitement might react.

No time for explanations came,
The program now had reached her name;
Then Agnes stood in robe of white,
Upon the platform to recite.

All eyes were riveted on her,
The vision caused a conscious stir;
For Agnes, whom they thought demure,
Was radiant now and brilliant sure.

GRADUATION.

Fair skinned by nature, and clear eyed,
By grief she was so sorely tried,
Her countenance translucent grew,
Till very soul was shining through.

" Fruition " was her theme that night;
She spoke as if inspired quite;
And though the burden of her thought,
Was to eternal issue brought,
She spoke with all the confidence,
Which knowledge gave for her defence.

Her teachers, friends, and parents, too,
With admiration watched her through.

She saw but one, in all that press,
To him she did her words address.

And he approached, now, at the end,
Congratulations to extend;
When to the great surprise of all,
Joe Manly's name did Agnes call.

She knew he surely would be there,
For once since that excursion rare,
Had Joe and Agnes meeting found,
At the appointed Indian Mound;
When Joe, to his amazement, heard
Of that dread charge 'gainst him preferred.

" It is a sad mistake," said he,
" Or else a base conspiracy.
But never, while I have my breath,
Shall Agnes share this living death.
I will the accusation meet,
And prove my innocence complete."

One favor only Joe had sought,—
That to his soul strength might be brought;—
That on her graduation day,
He might attend and tribute pay,
Of love, and admiration true,
As constant friends are wont to do.

And sadly then they had agreed,
To meet no more till Joe was freed.

And so it came about that night,
That Joe had reappeared to sight;
And thence was known to comrades fond,
As that strange *Hermit of Moss Pond*.

XV.

The Trial.

Suspense.

—Sonnet.—

LONG weary days, and longer sleepless nights,
Death's door upon its rusty hinges swung;
While smiles and tears each other chased among
The anxious watchers, in fantastic flights,
As now the portals closed on Pluto's blights,
Now creaking op'ed the yawning gulf, and flung
Fresh terrors into hearts with anguish wrung.
With doubtful issue the contending sprites,
Who Sentinel the pass 'twixt life and death,
Strove for the mastery, until at last
Again the door, from standing open wide,
Swung to, before the pitying angel's breath.
The latchet, quivering, at length fell fast,
And shut our darling on the *hither* side.

IV. The Trial.

WHEN Joe was made aware, at last,
    Of that suspicion o'er him cast;
He hastened to the county seat,
Where accusation he might meet;
Gave bail for court a few weeks hence,
And then prepared to make defence.

He surely could not understand,
Why they should him a felon brand;
And made resolve to shun Green Crest,
If this suspicion on him rest.

An honored man he was that day,
When he had gone from there away;
An honored man he would return,
Or else its confines he would spurn.

The day of trial was at hand;
What evidence he could command,

Had Joe prepared for his defence;
Then longed for trial to commence.

At last was Joe arraigned in court,
And asked to plead to the report
Which the Grand Jury had returned,
Soon after the default was learned.

Just what was charged Joe had not heard,
Till now in court the case occurred.

He knew that trust funds were involved,
To what extent he had not solved,—
Nor did it matter just how large.

The clerk then read to Joe the charge:

" You are indicted, on account
Of having taken large amount
Of funds, entrusted to your care,
While agent at Green Crest, last year.
Guilty or not? What do you plead?"

THE TRIAL.

"Not guilty," answered Joe, with speed.

The jury then was quickly drawn,
And ere the sun to rest had gone,
The people had their case outlined,
And in its meshes Joe entwined.

"Have you no counsel?" asked the court.
"None," answered Joe, "of legal sort;
But stand alone in my defense,
Supported by my evidence."

"Do you not wish for counsel, then?"
"None," quickly answered Joe, again.
"All I desire is that the court
Will just my legal rights support.
Sufficient load I have," he said,
"With this indictment o'er my head,
Without the ghost of legal fees,
To haunt me till I have no ease."

A sneering smile was seen to pass
O'er many a lawyer's guileless face;
But Joe knew well they could not save,
Unless his case the chances gave;
And if he could such chance present,
With jury he would be content.

The people's case was soon complete,
The web was like a winding sheet,
Till Joe seemed tangled in portents,
Without the shadow of defence.

The books were figured up in court,
The vouchers, too, read in support.

The tickets tallied to a jot,
Nor was the letter press forgot,
On which was traced in Joe's own hand,
The records which the funds demand.

Joe's disappearance was outlined,—
The action of a guilty mind.

All this was true, except the last,
Which Joe without objection passed.

Joe's turn now came, and first he called
The maid whose error we forestalled.

A crumpled letter he showed her.
" Now on your oath please to aver,
When first did you see this, and where?"

" 'Twas at the home of Henry Daire,
December twenty-fourth, last year."

" How is it thus to you so clear?"

" I must confess, my curious eyes
Made me both guilty and unwise.
I saw two letters, read them through,
And sent the wrong one then to you."

"So much," said Joe, "to thus explain
Why disappearance might be plain."

Next came the agent to the stand,
With all the books at his command.

The telegrams they then produce,
By which Joe had obtained excuse;
And one receipt upon the book,
The people's witness did o'er-look.

But there it was, in letters plain,
"Received, one package," signed, "J. Main."
The date, "December twenty-three,
On number four, bound east, G. C."

J. Main next took the witness stand.
Such interest he did command,
That deathly silence now prevailed,
As he his evidence detailed.

"I was a messenger," he said,
"But on that day I took my bed,
And there for months with fever tossed,
Until employment I had lost.
I have no recollection now,
But that receipt I must avow.
I was so ill when I arrived,
Report by proxy I contrived;
But of this package here concerned,
I never till this moment learned.
Why it was not with my report,
I surely cannot tell the court."

A close observer might have seen
Expressive nodding pass between
The jury, at this last display,
And at the close of that first day,
So changed the situation was,
For this opinion there was cause:
A verdict might be brought about,
For Joe, of reasonable doubt.

The jury now had filed away,
To be returned another day.

Then Joe at length addressed the court:
" For my defence, a good support,
One witness more I greatly need.
I pray for order, with some speed,
For the attendance here, straightway,
Of Mrs. Main; and if I may,
With '*duce tecum*,' for such things
As to her mind this notice brings."

He handed up the notice, then
Resumed his place at bar, again.

The judge reviewed the circumstance,
And saw with even casual glance,
If he this order should withhold,
' Twould only cause delay untold.

Here was foundation for defence
Of new discovered evidence.

THE TRIAL.

And if conviction be obtained,
On this indictment, as arraigned;
He clearly saw no other way,
Himself would have to grant a stay.

The order issued, and, next day
When court convened, a large array
Of curious people did attend,
To see how Joe's affairs would end.

Excitement ran the court room through,
When Mrs. Main came into view.

She took the stand and answers gave,
As Joe inquired with questions grave:

" I am the wife of witness Main,
And well remember with what pain
He reached his home, one day last year,
And lay with fever most severe,
For months, till life was quite despaired.
When fever left, was not prepared

His old employment to resume,
But sought some service nearer home."

" What kind of clothing did he wear,
When messenger on rail-way car ?"

" The customary uniform,
To which all messengers conform."

" Where were these garments put away
On that remote December day ?"

" In garret clothes-press they have been,
And not until this morning seen."

" Where are they now ?" said Joe, on fire
With interest, "if I may inquire."

" There in that satchel, somewhat large,
The officer has in his charge."

THE TRIAL.

" Will you examine carefully,
If aught in pockets you can see?"

The court and jury craned to look,
As Mrs. Main the satchel took;
And when the coat she had removed,
Joe's innocence was straightway proved;
For there the package was concealed,
Which this strange story has revealed.

The seal was broken; and intact
Was found the money, closely packed;
Full seven hundred dollars, too,
To the last cent from Joe then due.

The kindly judge, with moistened eyes,
Dismissed the jury in this wise:

" You, gentlemen, may be excused;
The prisoner has been abused;
And clearly nothing here remains,
For your considerative pains."

And then he bade poor Joe advance,
And took his hand, with kindly glance.

" You are forthwith discharged," he said;
Then placed his hand upon his head,—
" May grace attend. You may go now."

" Your Honor," broke in Mr. Howe,—
The high official of the road,
Whose countenance with pleasure glowed.
" Permit me here to undertake,
What reparation we may make."

" You take the package they produce,
And count these sums for instant use:"

" For that December salary,
Full pay, with interest, we agree."

" And thence, until this very day,
As compensation, count half-pay."

THE TRIAL.

And then to Joe he quickly turned,
" Our meek apologies you've earned.
Our best position now at hand,
Will gladly be at your command.
Or, if your interests elsewhere lay,
Here is a 'pass,' time, without day."

The court adjourned, and then the wire,
This message flashed to Agnes Daire:

" You may expect me, glad and free;
I will arrive on number three."

XVI.
Fruition.

Away at School.

Sonnet.

AWAY at school! "God bless our children dear."
  At each returning, sad, lone eventide,
    Up from devout home altars far and wide,
Ascends the fervent prayer; while hope and fear
Alternate in the mind, as year by year,
  Relentless time, to alchemy allied,
    Unconsciously transmeets our household's pride,
From childhood's playful moods, to manhood's sphere.

As they this transient life most nobly spend,
  Who cankering self-indulgence least desire,
    Parental hearts, with love almost divine,
With pure self-sacrifice their treasures lend,
  To eruditions all refining fire,
    Though ne'er again the casket all confine.

LVI. Fruition.

THREE years have passed, and Christmas eve
Some new attention must receive.

The church was vacant, at Green Crest;
A call was recently addressed
To Reverend Joseph Manly, late
A Hartwick cleric graduate,
And his acceptance was at hand.

His installation had been planned
For Sabbath evening; which, that year,
Was Christmas eve, as will appear.

The President of Synod then,
With his assistant clergymen,
Had solemnly the service read,
Which did the church and pastor wed.
The youthful pastor then retired,
Their pride,—by every eye admired.

The President then smiling said:
" One other pair must now be wed."

Joe Manly neared the altar stair,
And on his arm leaned Agnes Daire;

And then was heard the plighted vow:—
Her name is Agnes Manly now.